HOMEWOOD PUBLIC LIBRARY DISTRICT

P9-ELO-320

3 1311 00324 5188

TYRANNOSAURUS REX

By Susan H. Gray

THE CHILD'S WORLD®

CHA............ESOTA

HOMEWOOD PUBLIC LIBRARY

JUN   2004

Published in the United States of America by The Child's World®
P.O. Box 326, Chanhassen, MN 55317-0326
800-599-READ
www.childsworld.com

Content Adviser:
Peter Makovicky,
Ph.D., Curator,
Field Museum,
Chicago, Illinois

Photo Credits: American Museum of Natural History Library: 13 (#19508); 15 (#315293, Thane Bierwert); Royalty-Free/Corbis: 6; Tony Arruza/Corbis: 10; Corbis: 11, 17 bottom; Bettmann/Corbis: 14; AFP/Corbis: 16; Reuters NewMedia, Inc./Corbis: 18; Annie Poole, Papilio/Corbis: 24; Richard T. Nowitz/Corbis: 27; AFP/Getty Images: 8; Hulton|Archive/Getty Images: 12; Gary Retherford/Photo Researchers, Inc.: 7; Chris Butler/Science Photo Library/Photo Researchers, Inc.: 20–21; John Eastcott, Yva Momatiuk/Photo Researchers, Inc.: 22; Mark Garlick/Science Photo Library/ Photo Researchers, Inc.: 26; Mark Gibson/Visuals Unlimited, Inc.: 5; A.J. Copley/ Visuals Unlimited, Inc.: 9; Ken Lucas/Visuals Unlimited, Inc.: 17 top.

The Child's World®: Mary Berendes, Publishing Director

Editorial Directions, Inc.: E. Russell Primm, Editorial Director; Dana Meachen Rau, Line Editor; Katie Marsico, Assistant Editor; Matthew Messbarger, Editorial Assistant; Susan Hindman, Copy Editor; Susan Ashley, Proofreader; Tim Griffin, Indexer; Kerry Reid, Fact Checker; Dawn Friedman, Photo Reseacher; Linda S. Koutris, Photo Selector

Original cover art by Todd Marshall

The Design Lab: Kathleen Petelinsek, Design and Page Production

Copyright © 2004 by The Child's World®
All rights reserved. No part of this book may be reproduced or utilized in any form or by any means without written permission from the publisher.

Library of Congress Cataloging-in-Publication Data
Gray, Susan Heinrichs.
 Tyrannosaurus rex / by Susan H. Gray.
   p. cm. — (Exploring dinosaurs)
Includes index.
Summary: Describes what is known about the physical characteristics, behavior, habitat, and life cycle of this massive flesh-eating dinosaur.
 ISBN 1-59296-046-4 (lib. bdg. : alk. paper)
 1. Tyrannosaurus rex—Juvenile literature. [1. Tyrannosaurus rex. 2. Dinosaurs.] I. Title. II. Series.
QE862.S3G6957
2004 567.912'9—dc22   2003018633

TABLE OF CONTENTS

CHAPTER ONE

4 A Feast Fit for a King

CHAPTER TWO

7 What Is a *Tyrannosaurus Rex?*

CHAPTER THREE

13 Who Found the First *Tyrannosaurus Rex?*

CHAPTER FOUR

19 Mighty Hunter or Not?

CHAPTER FIVE

23 Another Mystery

CHAPTER SIX

25 A Short-Timer

28 Glossary

28 Did You Know?

29 The Geologic Time Scale

30 How to Learn More

32 Index

A Feast Fit
for a King

The sun was setting, and evening shadows slowly stretched

across the land. A few birds crossed the sky on their way

home. Soft breezes rustled through the oak trees. Only one sound

cut through the calm—the sound of *Tyrannosaurus rex* (tie-RAN-uh-

SORE-uhss REX) eating.

A dead *Triceratops* (try-SEHR-uh-tops) lay at his feet. With his

daggerlike teeth, *Tyrannosaurus rex* tore a mouthful of flesh from the

animal's side. He swallowed the 50 pounds (22.7 kilograms) of meat

in one gulp.

The claws on his front legs grasped the air as he ate. His tail

swung heavily each time he bent down for another bite. Every few

minutes, the dinosaur stopped and looked up. He sniffed the air and

A replica of Tyrannosaurus rex *eating a* Triceratops. Triceratops *had a bony plate along the back of its skull and three sharp horns on its head for protection against enemies. Unfortunately for* Triceratops, Tyrannosaurus rex *had razor-sharp teeth that could wound and kill another dinosaur with one ferocious bite.*

Tyrannosaurus rex probably stopped and sniffed the air to sense if other dinosaurs were near. Scientists know that a large area of a Tyrannosaurus's brain was used for processing certain smells. This sharp sense of smell undoubtedly helped the dinosaur track down its dinner.

paused. Then he went back to his bloody meal.

Finally, with his stomach full and his sides bulging, he stopped eating. He might not have another meal for days, or even weeks. But this was enough for now. He headed off, searching for the perfect place to nap.

CHAPTER TWO

WHAT IS A TYRANNOSAURUS REX?

Tyrannosaurus rex, or *T. rex* for short, is a dinosaur that lived about 67 million to 65 million years ago. The name *Tyranno-saurus* is taken from Greek words that mean "tyrant lizard." *Rex* is from a Latin word that means "king." It was given this name because scientists believed *T. rex* was a fierce dinosaur that could defeat all others.

A large adult *T. rex* reached 40 feet (12.2 meters) in length. It weighed as much as 6 or 7 tons. *T. rex*

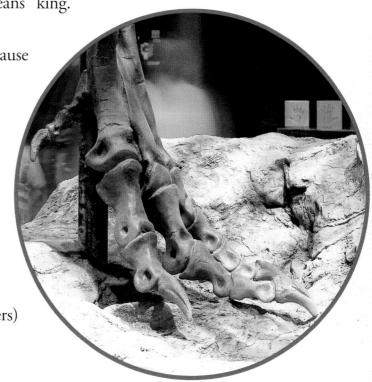

T. rex had powerful limbs with dangerously sharp nails. If T. rex had a victim grasped in its jaws, it could rip into the animal's flesh with the claws on its birdlike hands and feet.

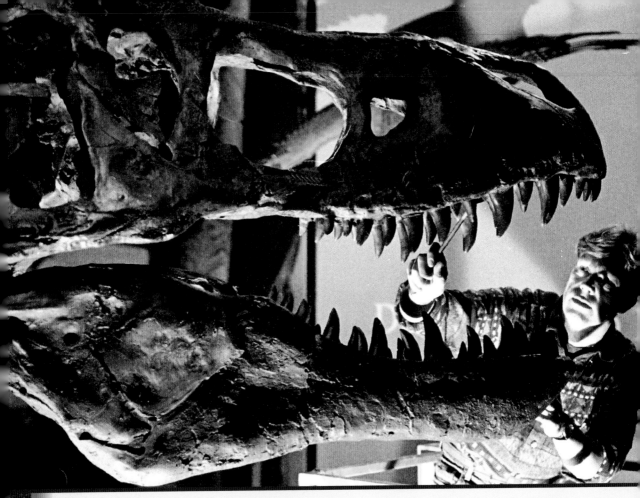

A scientist examines the skull of a T. rex. *The brain that once existed inside this large skull gave* T. rex *the reputation of being among the more intelligent dinosaurs of its time.*

had an enormous skull, up to 5 feet (1.5 m) long. Each eye was almost

the size of a baseball. The dinosaur probably had very good eyesight

and a strong sense of smell.

T. rex walked on two mighty legs. Its feet ended in three clawed

toes. A smaller claw, the dewclaw, stuck out in back. Each front limb

Because T. rex *was always losing old teeth and growing new ones, it had teeth of several different sizes in its mouth at any given moment. Unfortunately for the animals it hunted, this didn't make* T. rex's *bite any less powerful!*

was about the size of a man's arm. These limbs were tiny for a **reptile** of this size, but they were strong and powerful. Each one ended in two clawed fingers.

Its jaws were filled with more than 50 teeth, some up to 1 foot (30.5 centimeters) long. Throughout the dinosaur's life, new teeth

A view of the tail on a T. rex *statue in Daytona Beach, Florida. Only one* T. rex *skeleton has been found with a virtually complete tail.*

constantly grew in. As each old tooth tore out or fell out, another grew in its place. The creature had a thick, muscular neck and powerful jaw muscles. Its bite could easily crush bone.

T. rex had a thick, heavy tail. It probably acted as a balance for its huge head. As *T. rex* walked, the dinosaur held its tail stiff and off the ground.

HOW DO WE KNOW ABOUT DINOSAURS?

Today, we know all kinds of things about dinosaurs. We know they lived millions of years ago. We have found fossils they left behind— their bones, eggs, footprints, and even their droppings. But in the past, people knew nothing about dinosaurs. When they found dinosaur bones, they thought they were from animals much like those of today.

Robert Plot was a scientist who lived in England in the 1600s. He found a leg bone from a big, meat-eating dinosaur. The bone was so huge it puzzled Plot for a long time. He thought that it was either the thighbone of a giant man or a bone from an elephant. Even though he was wrong, he was the first scientist to write about such a find.

Over the years, more mysterious bones were found. Scientists wondered what kinds of animals they came from. Some thought they might be from huge rhinoceroses. Others thought they might be from giant crocodiles.

Finally, another English scientist, Sir Richard Owen, came up with a new idea. He said the unusual bones were from a completely different group of animals. In 1842, he named this group the dinosaurs. The name means "terrifying lizards." Today, scientists know that dinosaurs are not lizards. And some were not terrifying at all.

CHAPTER THREE

WHO FOUND THE FIRST TYRANNOSAURUS REX?

Barnum Brown, a famous dinosaur hunter, was the first to find a *T. rex* skeleton. He spotted it in 1902 in Montana.

He was looking for bones of other dinosaurs. Instead, he found the

hips, hind legs, and a few other pieces of a completely new dinosaur.

Barnum Brown in 1902. In addition to finding the first T. rex *skeleton, Brown was responsible for naming several dinosaurs, such as* Ankylosaurus.

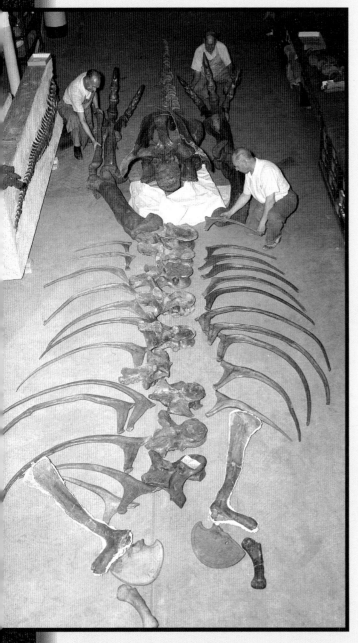

Fossils can often be easily damaged or broken. Many early scientists weren't aware of this and ended up losing valuable dinosaur bones by handling them roughly. Above, Brown and his team exercise caution as they put together the skeleton of a T. rex *in 1942.*

From the bones he found, he could tell that this new dinosaur was enormous.

The bones were firmly embedded in rock. Brown and his team of workers took two summers to dig them out of the surrounding rock. They packed up the bones and sent them by train to the American Museum of Natural History in New York City. There, scientists worked for years cleaning the bones and putting the skeleton together. In 1905, the museum boss, Henry Osborn, gave it the name *Tyrannosaurus rex.* One of the workers said the dinosaur's "smile" made it look like President Teddy Roosevelt. He called the animal Teddysaurus as a joke.

The new dinosaur was instantly popular. People came from miles around to see it. Magazines ran stories about the creature. Its picture appeared in newspapers all over the country.

A T. rex *skeleton at the American Museum of Natural History in New York. The original* T. rex *skeleton Brown discovered was first housed at this museum, but was later moved to the Carnegie Museum in Pittsburgh, Pennsylvania, where it remains today.*

Sue Hendrickson with her discovery at the Field Museum in Chicago, Illinois. Some of her other famous finds include fossilized whales from ancient times and sunken treasure at the bottom of rivers and oceans.

Meanwhile, Brown kept looking for more *T. rex* remains. In time, he found enough bones to know what the whole skeleton looked like. Since then, many people have looked for *T. rex* bones.

In 1990, fossil hunter Sue Hendrickson found a huge *T. rex* in South Dakota. It was nicknamed "Sue" after her. No one really knows, however, whether it was male or female.

A DINO NAMED SUE

Paleontologists (PAY-lee-un-TAWL-uh-jists) were thrilled when they heard about Sue, the *T. rex.* Paleontologists are people who study ancient forms of plant and animal life. Sue was certainly ancient—probably around 67 million years old. She was the biggest *T. rex* ever found. And with more than 200 bones, she was also the most complete.

Sue was sold to a museum in Chicago, Illinois. There, skilled workers cleaned and repaired her bones. The job took more than 25,000 hours!

Next, a group of experts figured out how the skele-

ton would be supported, or held in place. A skeleton cannot stand by itself. It needs screws, wires, and rods to hold it up. Proper support takes lots of planning.

Together, scientists and artists figured out how Sue should pose. Engineers had to agree that the pose would work. Then they designed her support system. Museum workers built a little model of Sue and her supports. Adjustments were made here and there. Then blacksmiths and metal workers started building the real supports. They even called in a jewelry maker to help. Everything had to be just right. Thousands of hours later, Sue was ready to face her museum visitors.

CHAPTER FOUR

MIGHTY HUNTER
OR NOT?

When *Tyrannosaurus rex* first became popular, everyone was sure it was a vicious hunter. Henry Osborn said it was true. The newspapers and magazines all said so. But today, scientists are not so certain. After looking at the animal's head, body, and footprints, they are giving this dinosaur more thought. Maybe *T. rex* ran down its **prey** and tore it to shreds. But maybe not.

Scientists have tried to figure out how fast *T. rex* could run by comparing the size of its leg bones to those of living animals. Today, many scientists think the animal could run between 10 and 25 miles (16.1 and 40.2 kilometers) an hour. This is much slower than the speeding *T. rex* often shown in movies.

T. rex's huge head is also a problem. If

T. rex really raced after prey, it would have

had to stay perfectly balanced. Otherwise,

the heavy head would cause the dinosaur

to topple over and crash. No **predator**

would last long doing that!

The legs also confused scientists.

Although *Tyrannosaurus rex* had very

strong, muscular legs, this does not mean

it was a swift runner. The rest of the ani-

mal's body was huge, too. *T. rex* would

have needed much bigger legs to carry that

huge body around quickly.

Scientists also puzzle over those little

Artwork showing T. rex racing after its prey. Part of the reason scientists began to wonder whether T. rex could be so speedy is because big animals generally don't move very fast.

This model of T. rex *shows its tiny arms. Some scientists feel the claws could be used for ripping into a victim. Most agree, however, that* T. rex *probably had to grip an animal with its jaws before the arms could tear it apart.*

arms. They seem too small and close to the body to hold and tear

prey. Scientists are not sure exactly what they were for.

All these things seem to say that *T. rex* was not a fierce hunter.

Some paleontologists think it just attacked old, sick, or weak animals.

Or perhaps it ate animals that were already dead. Maybe it hunted a

little and **scavenged** a little. We may never know the answer.

CHAPTER FIVE

ANOTHER MYSTERY

For years, scientists have wondered whether dinosaurs were warm-blooded or cold-blooded. Warm-blooded animals keep about the same body temperature no matter what the weather is like. Human beings are warm-blooded, for example. It does not matter whether they work outside in the heat or go sledding in the snow. Their bodies try to keep their temperature at about 98.6° Fahrenheit (37° Celsius).

Cold-blooded animals are very different. Their temperatures go up and down with the temperature of their **environment**. Fish, reptiles, and amphibians are cold-blooded. Such animals tend to move more slowly when their temperature drops. They also stay out of the hot sun to keep from becoming too warm.

Of course, we cannot study living dinosaurs. So we do not know whether these creatures were warm-blooded or cold-blooded. Some scientists think that *T. rex* was a warm-blooded animal. They believe that birds are related to dinosaurs. Because birds are warm-blooded, maybe dinosaurs were warm-blood-

This little lizard is a cold-blooded animal. Even in captivity, lizards need an outside source of heat or light so they can keep their body temperature from dropping too low. That is why people who own them as pets often have rocks that produce warmth or special lamps that allow the lizards to bask in artificial light.

ed. Other scientists think that *T. rex* was cold-blooded. After all, *T. rex* was a reptile and reptiles are cold-blooded. This is just one more mystery that scientists are working to solve.

CHAPTER SIX

A Short-Timer

The first dinosaurs appeared about 225 million years ago.

Dinosaurs walked the Earth for the next 160 million years. The animals changed over long periods of time. New kinds of dinosaurs appeared. Older kinds died out. About 65 million years ago, however, all of the dinosaurs disappeared. *Tyrannosaurus rex* appeared just a few million years before all the dinosaurs became extinct. Even if *T. rex* was the "king" of the dinosaurs, it ruled on Earth for only a short time.

Paleontologists are not sure what wiped out all the dinosaurs. Some say the Earth became too hot or too cold. Some believe that volcanoes were the problem. Their dust and ash filled the air and darkened the skies.

If an asteroid did hit Earth, the entire food chain would have been affected. Plants depend on sunlight to survive, so they probably would have died first. With nothing to eat, plant eaters would have become extinct, and then meat eaters such as T. rex would have died from lack of prey to hunt.

Today, many scientists believe a giant asteroid slammed into the Earth. The crash was so big that it sent dirt and ash flying for thousands of miles. It blocked out sunlight, and plants and animals died.

We do not know if this is really what killed the dinosaurs. But we do know they all became **extinct** at about the same time.

There are many mysteries surrounding *T. rex* and the other

dinosaurs. We may never solve them all. But we will find answers to

some of them. Every year, paleontologists find more fossils left by

these creatures. Each fossil brings us closer to understanding how

they lived and how they died.

Paleontologists at work. Scientists will continue to search for more T. rex *fossils. Only about 30 have been discovered so far, but who knows how many more are waiting to be found?*

Glossary

ancient (AYN-shunt) Something that is ancient is very old; from millions of years ago. Paleontologists study ancient forms of plant and animal life.

environment (en-VYE-ruhn-muhnt) An environment is made up of the things that surround a living creature, such as the air and soil. The temperature of cold blood-ed animals depends upon the temperature of the environment around them.

extinct (ek-STINGKT) Something that is extinct has died out and is no longer in exis-tence. The dinosaurs are now all extinct.

fossils (FOSS-uhlz) Fossils are the things left behind by an ancient plant or ani-mal. People can often view dinosaur fossils in museums.

predator (PRED-uh-tur) A predator is an animal that hunts and eats other animals. As a predator, *T. rex* couldn't chase other animals at high speeds because of the size of its enormous head.

prey (PRAY) Prey is an animal that is hunted and eaten by other animals. Scientists wonder how *T. rex* used its small arms to hunt and catch prey.

reptile (REP-tile) A reptile is an air-breathing animal with a backbone and is usually covered with scales or plates. *T. rex* was a reptile.

scavenged (SKAV-uhnjd) Scavenged describes the process of eating something that is already dead. *T. rex* may have hunted and scav-enged to find its food.

Did You Know?

▶ In 1998, the first nearly complete skeleton of a young *Tyrannosaurus rex* was found in South Dakota.

▶ Scientists believe that *T. rex* could smell and see very well because the dinosaur's brain had very large areas for these two senses.

▶ In the 1940s, a museum paid $7,000 for a *Tyrannosaurus rex* skeleton. In the 1990s, another museum paid more than $8 million for Sue.

The Geologic Time Scale

TRIASSIC PERIOD

Date: 248 million to 208 million years ago

Fossils: *Coelophysis, Cynodont, Desmatosuchus, Eoraptor, Gerrothorax, Peteinosaurus, Placerias, Plateosaurus, Postosuchus, Procompsognathus, Riojasaurus, Saltopus, Teratosaurus, Thecodontosaurus*

Distinguishing Features: For the most part, the climate in the Triassic period was hot and dry. The first true mammals appeared during this period, as well as turtles, frogs, salamanders, and lizards. Corals could also be found in oceans at this time, although large reefs such as the ones we have today did not yet exist. Evergreen trees made up much of the plant life.

JURASSIC PERIOD

Date: 208 million to 144 million years ago

Fossils: *Allosaurus, Anchisaurus, Apatosaurus, Barosaurus, Brachiosaurus, Ceratosaurus, Compsognathus, Cryptoclidus, Dilophosaurus, Diplodocus, Eustreptospondylus, Hybodus, Janenschia, Kentrosaurus, Liopleurodon, Megalosaurus, Opthalmosaurus, Rhamphorhynchus, Saurolophus, Segisaurus, Seismosaurus, Stegosaurus, Supersaurus, Syntarsus, Ultrasaurus, Vulcanodon, Xiaosaurus*

Distinguishing Features: The climate of the Jurassic period was warm and moist. The first birds appeared during this period. Plant life was also greener and more widespread. Sharks began swimming in Earth's oceans. Although dinosaurs didn't even exist at the beginning of the Triassic period, they ruled Earth by Jurassic times. There was a minor mass extinction toward the end of the Jurassic period.

CRETACEOUS PERIOD

Date: 144 million to 65 million years ago

Fossils: *Acrocanthosaurus, Alamosaurus, Albertosaurus, Anatotitan, Ankylosaurus, Argentinosaurus, Bagaceratops, Baryonyx, Carcharodontosaurus, Carnotaurus, Centrosaurus, Chasmosaurus, Corythosaurus, Didelphodon, Edmontonia, Edmontosaurus, Gallimimus, Gigantosaurus, Hadrosaurus, Hypsilophodon, Iguanodon, Kronosaurus, Lambeosaurus, Leaellynasaura, Maiasaura, Megaraptor, Muttaburrasaurus, Nodosaurus, Ornithocheirus, Oviraptor, Pachycephalosaurus, Panoplosaurus, Parasaurolophus, Pentaceratops, Polacanthus, Protoceratops, Psittacosaurus, Quaesitosaurus, Saltasaurus, Sarcosuchus, Saurolophus, Sauropelta, Saurornithoides, Segnosaurus, Spinosaurus, Stegoceras, Stygimoloch, Styracosaurus, Tapejara, Tarbosaurus, Therizinosaurus, Thescelosaurus, Torosaurus, Trachodon, Triceratops, Troodon, Tyrannosaurus rex, Utahraptor, Velociraptor*

Distinguishing Features: The climate of the Cretaceous period was fairly mild. Flowering plants first appeared in this period, and many modern plants developed. With flowering plants came a greater diversity of insect life. Birds further developed into two types: flying and flightless. A wider variety of mammals also existed. At the end of this period came a great mass extinction that wiped out the dinosaurs, along with several other groups of animals.

How to Learn More

At the Library

Hartzog, Brooke. *Tyrannosaurus Rex and Barnum Brown.*
New York: PowerKids Press, 1999.

Relf, Patricia.
A Dinosaur Named Sue: The Story of the Colossal Fossil: The World's Most Complete T. Rex.
New York: Scholastic Trade, 2000.

On the Web

Visit our home page for lots of links about *Tyrannosaurus rex:*
http://www.childsworld.com/links.html
Note to Parents, Teachers, and Librarians: We routinely verify our
Web links to make sure they're safe, active sites—so encourage
your readers to check them out!

Places to Visit or Contact

AMERICAN MUSEUM OF NATURAL HISTORY
To view numerous dinosaur fossils, as well as
the fossils of several ancient mammals
Central Park West at 79th Street
New York, NY 10024-5192
212/769-5100

CARNEGIE MUSEUM OF NATURAL HISTORY
To view a variety of dinosaur skeletons, as well as fossils related
to other reptiles, amphibians, and fish that are now extinct
4400 Forbes Avenue
Pittsburgh, PA 15213
412/622-3131

DINOSAUR NATIONAL MONUMENT
To view a huge deposit of dinosaur bones in a natural setting
4545 East Highway 40
Dinosaur, CO 81610-9724

or

DINOSAUR NATIONAL MONUMENT (QUARRY)
11625 East 1500 South
Jensen, UT 84035
435/781-7700

FIELD MUSEUM OF NATURAL HISTORY
To see the dinosaur named Sue
1400 South Lake Shore Drive
Chicago, IL 60605-2496
312/922-9410

MUSEUM OF THE ROCKIES
To see real dinosaur fossils, as well as robotic replicas
Montana State University
600 West Kagy Boulevard
Bozeman, MT 59717-2730
406/994-2251 or 406/994-DINO (3466)

NATIONAL MUSEUM OF NATURAL HISTORY
(SMITHSONIAN INSTITUTION)
To see several dinosaur exhibits and special behind-the-scenes tours
10th Street and Constitution Avenue, N.W.
Washington, DC 20560-0166
202/357-2700

Index

arms, 8–9, 20–22
asteroid, 26, 27

birds, 24
bones, 11–12, 17, 19. *See also* skeleton.
Brown, Barnum, 13, 14, 16

claws, 4, 8, 9
cold-blooded animals, 23–24

dewclaw, 8

extinction, 25–26
eyes, 8

food, 4, 6, 19, 20, 22
fossils, 11, 27

head, 8, 10, 20
Hendrickson, Sue, 16

jaw, 9, 10

legs, 4, 8, 19, 20

name, 7, 15
neck, 10

Osborn, Henry, 15, 19
Owen, Sir Richard, 12

paleontologists, 17, 22, 25, 27
Plot, Robert, 11
prey, 19, 20, 22

reptiles, 9, 23, 24

size, 7
skeleton, 13–14, 16, 18. *See also* bones.
skull, 8
"Sue," 16, 17–18

tail, 4, 10
teeth, 9–10
toes, 8
Triceratops, 4

warm-blooded animals, 23–24
weight, 7

About the Author

Susan H. Gray has bachelor's and master's degrees in zoology, and has taught college-level courses in biology. She first fell in love with fossil hunting while studying paleontology in college. In her 25 years as an author, she has written many articles for scientists and researchers, and many science books for children. Susan enjoys gardening, traveling, and playing the piano. She and her husband, Michael, live in Cabot, Arkansas.